undressed

Edwina Ehrman

undressed
A Brief History of Underwear

V&A Publishing

This book presents highlights from the Victoria and Albert Museum's exhibition *Undressed: A Brief History of Underwear*. The displays encompass men's and women's underclothes from about 1750 to the present and garments which have been influenced by underwear or developed from it. The majority were designed, made and worn in Britain, Europe and North America.

The exhibition *Undressed: A Brief History of Underwear* (16 April 2016–12 March 2017) is sponsored by

First published by V&A Publishing, 2015
Victoria and Albert Museum
South Kensington
London SW7 2RL
www.vandapublishing.com

ISBN 9781 85177 885 0

10 9 8 7 6 5 4 3 2 1
2020 2019 2018 2017 2016

Designer: Maggi Smith

New photography by Jaron James, V&A Photographic Studio

Printed in China

V&A Publishing

Supporting the world's leading museum of art and design, the Victoria and Albert Museum, London

Front cover illustration
Corset
Silk satin, lace and whalebone
with a steel busk and metal eyelets
Probably Britain, 1890–5
V&A: T.738–1974

Back cover illustration
**Fig leaf for the cast of *David*,
after the marble original by
Michelangelo (1475–1564),
probably made by
D. Brucciani & Co.**
Plaster
Probably Britain, c.1857
V&A: REPRO.1857A–161

Frontispiece
Boudoir bodice
Silk satin, machine-made lace,
whalebone and metal eyelets,
trimmed with silk satin ribbon
France, c.1905
V&A: T.340–1978

Page 6
**Energy bra designed by
lululemon athletica**
Luxtreme and Lycra
Canada (Vancouver), 2015

391.
423
EHR

MIX
Paper from
responsible sources
FSC® C019910

Contents

Sponsors' Forewords   7

Introduction   9

CHAPTER 1 **Hygiene and Comfort**   13

CHAPTER 2 **Shapeshifters**   41

CHAPTER 3 **Lingerie and Hosiery**   67

CHAPTER 4 **Revelation and Transformation**   95

Further Reading   110

Picture Credits   111

Acknowledgements   112

Sponsors' Forewords

Agent Provocateur is extremely proud to be involved in this innovative exhibition that celebrates the wonderful and powerful world of underwear. Since opening its first boutique in 1994 to becoming a globally recognized brand, Agent Provocateur has broken new ground and earned its place as a benchmark brand in the world of lingerie. Our unique brand image is renowned for being provocative while always leaving something to the imagination. We celebrate the empowerment of women under the creative direction of Sarah Shotton, a member of the design team since the company's launch. We hope that this exhibition inspires you!

Agent Provocateur

With over 80 years' experience revolutionizing the beauty industry and allowing women to express their most glamorous and amorous selves, Revlon are thrilled to be a sponsor of the exhibition *Undressed: A Brief History of Underwear*. As a brand, Revlon aims to inspire and embolden women to choose love, to act not wait, to do not dream. Because when you choose love, the outcome far exceeds what you imagined: your world is forever changed, and the possibilities are endless. We could not be more excited to work alongside brands within the exhibition that share both our heritage and vision to empower and celebrate women.

REVLON
LOVE IS ON

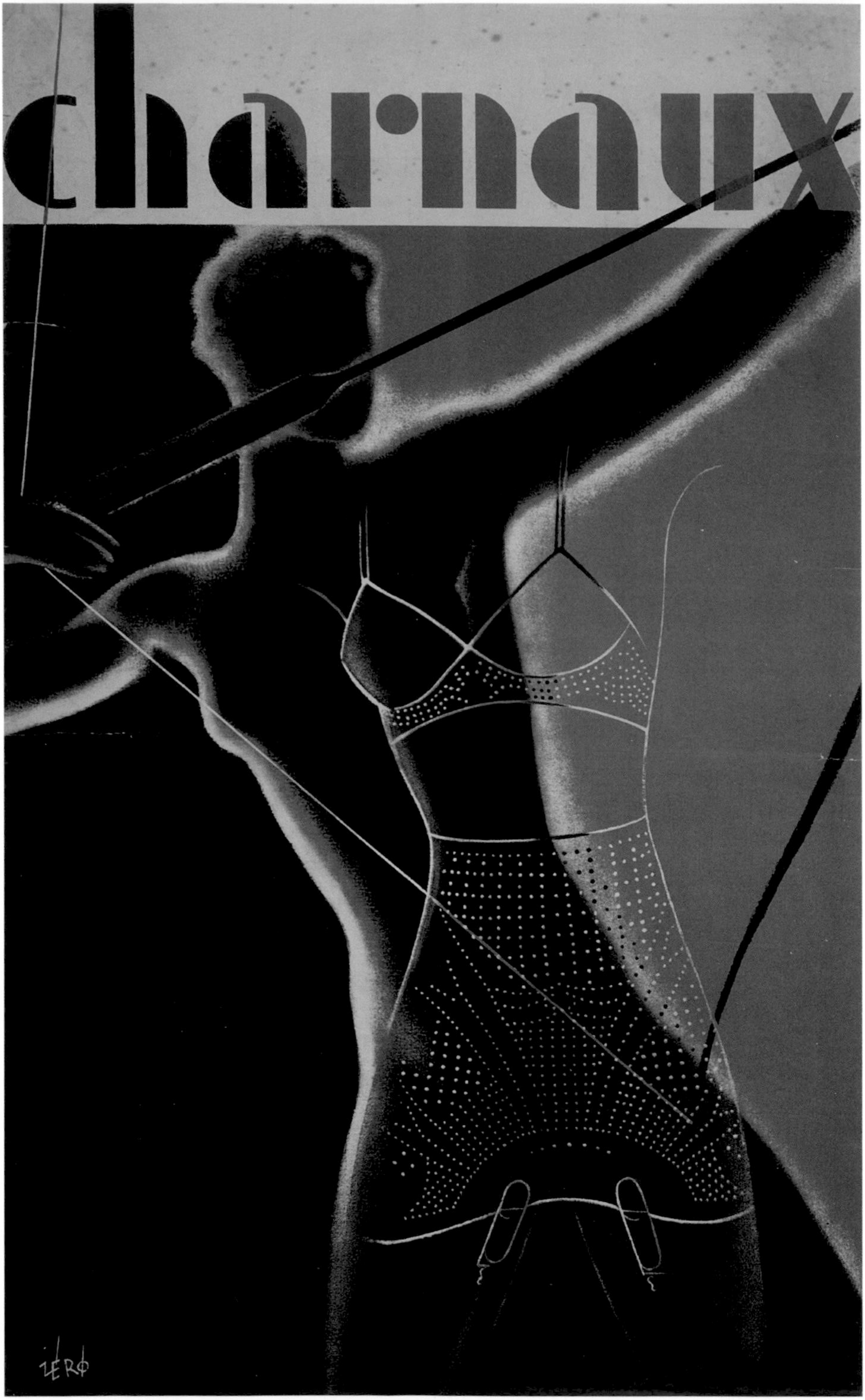
charnaux
ZERO

Introduction

Underclothes are the most personal garments in our wardrobe. Worn next to the skin and usually hidden, even the most practical garments are intrinsically erotic. There is always a possibility that they may be seen, accidentally or by design. Their cut, fit, fabric and decoration reflect changing social and cultural attitudes to gender, sex and morality; shifting notions of public and private; and innovations in fabric technology and design. Definitions of underwear have also altered. Until the twentieth century, for example, men's shirts were categorized as underwear. It was considered bad manners to expose the sleeves, but displaying freshly laundered cuffs and a decorative shirtfront demonstrated the wearer's income and privileged lifestyle.

Underwear has several roles. It is worn for modesty, cleanliness and comfort, to conceal, protect and support the intimate parts of the anatomy. Some garments, such as corsets and contemporary shape wear, have a structural role determined by the day's fashionable silhouette or ideal body shape. Others, such as the delicate, feminine underclothes and nightwear described since the late nineteenth century as lingerie, are designed to be flattering and alluring. However, fashionable underwear has its detractors. The dress reformers of the nineteenth century argued against it on hygienic, economic and aesthetic grounds, and today there is a movement against underwear that is perceived as perpetuating gender stereotypes. Our individual choices reflect our identity, lifestyle, taste, desires and fantasies.

Little is known about most of the underwear in the V&A's collection but the skilful alterations and careful repairs found in many pieces suggest their value and perhaps their sensory and emotional significance for the wearers. While a few garments are hardly worn, the fabric of others has become soft, supple and comfortable through regular washing. Some garments are embroidered with initials or names, giving their original owners a ghostly presence.

Lingerie is often preserved for sentimental reasons or because of its high original cost. It was traditionally part of a woman's trousseau, the clothes and linen prepared before marriage for her new life. Often handmade, the best examples draw on exceptional craft skills and the finest fabrics.

Until the mid-twentieth century, many items of underwear were made at home by female family members, servants and itinerant needlewomen. Patterns for home dressmaking were available in books, periodicals, by mail order and, by the mid-nineteenth century, from specialist pattern shops. People on low incomes without the resources to make clothes bought from second-hand dealers and outfitters offering cheap ready-to-wear.

Today, shopping online for underwear is increasingly popular because of the number of styles and sizes readily available; buying by post was common in the past. In the eighteenth century, customers had to send their measurements or a garment to be copied. This method was superseded in the next century by the widespread distribution of catalogues by outfitters, department stores and specialists – The Jaeger Sanitary Woollen Company and other 'rational' underwear retailers whose customers believed in dress reform included. Changing rooms were also introduced, making personal shopping more attractive and phasing out the practice of tradesmen visiting clients at home.

The ready-made underwear industry grew steadily throughout the nineteenth century. Technological developments in textile production increased the range of accessibly priced materials. Manufacturers also benefited from Greenwood & Batley's band knife (1860), which, unlike scissors, could cut through many layers of cloth, making the sewing machine more commercially viable. Companies who worked from factories, rather than employing outworkers, could utilize steam power.

As underwear manufacturers proliferated, the market became more competitive. Individuals and companies applied for patents for inventions and, from 1839, copyright on designs. Many women in Britain and the United States were active inventors, particularly in the field of corsetry and, from the last quarter of the nineteenth century, in the design of bust supporters (the forerunner of the brassiere). Roxey Ann Caplin (1793–1888), who won a prize medal for her corsets at the Great Exhibition in 1851, was both an inventor and a writer. She promoted the importance of exercise for women's health alongside her designs.

Manufacturers also competed to find new materials that could shape and support the body. Tightly coiled metal wire, introduced for garters in about 1791, was used for corsets such as Henry Adcock's men's belts. However, after 1844, when the process of vulcanization (which reduced the impact of temperature changes on rubber) was patented, elastic was gradually introduced in underwear. Available only in short lengths it was used for shoulder straps and laces. This changed in 1931 with the introduction of Lastex. Made with an extruded latex core wrapped in cotton, rayon or silk, its supremacy was unchallenged until 1958 when DuPont patented Spandex, a synthetic stretch fibre produced from polyurethane. The continuing research into high-performance fabrics remains critical to the development of new products in the underwear and sportswear industries.

Underwear advertising offers an insight into consumer concerns identified by manufacturers, though these must be treated with caution. Nineteenth-century marketing focused on the health benefits of products, their durability and the comfort they offered. While these advertisements relied on text and simple woodcuts, marketing in the following centuries used fashion illustration and, increasingly from the 1950s, photography. Whether selling male or female underclothes, advertisements generally target both sexes as potential purchasers, spectators or wearers. Most play to the appeal of a youthful, fit, sexually attractive body, and the pleasure and anticipation of looking and feeling good.

The use of men and women as models inevitably encourages consumers to compare themselves (and their partners) to ideal, often unrealistic body types. The celebrity endorsement of brands has taken this a stage further while proving a very effective marketing tool. Both men and women are objectified in this process, but some companies now employ marketing that avoids hypersexualized images and foregrounds the garment.

CHAPTER I

Hygiene and Comfort

Shirt and drawers
Linen
Britain (shirt) and France (drawers),
1775–1800
V&A: T.360–1984; T.608–1996

Underwear helps keep the body clean, healthy and comfortable. Linen and (from the nineteenth century) cotton were worn against the skin because they could be laundered at high temperatures. Body linen protected expensive clothing from perspiration and grease, and the body from harmful dyes and ingrained dirt in hard-to-clean materials. Natural fibres can also regulate body temperature. Dr Jäeger (1832–1917) promoted the use of wool for its ability to facilitate perspiration and maintain an even temperature. Aertex, a cellular cotton fabric that also possesses these characteristics, has been in production since 1888.

Easy-care fabrics were introduced in the twentieth century, with materials such as the cellulosic fibre Celanese available from c.1919. Today, high performance fabrics like Tactel, made from nylon, bring comfort and functionality to underwear, while more sustainable fibres, like bamboo, answer contemporary environmental concerns.

Until the bra was introduced in the early twentieth century, corsets were worn by women of all classes to contain the breasts, provide support and ensure respectability. They were also recommended for various medical conditions and to improve posture; many manufacturers offered orthopaedic corsets.

While corsets played a hygienic role, designs for nightwear were born from the desire for comfort. Dressing gowns, for example, were worn at home during the day in the eighteenth and nineteenth centuries. Towards the end of the 1800s men's dressing gowns morphed into smoking suits and women's into tea gowns. Pyjamas were also versatile and worn for home entertaining throughout the 1920s and 1930s. They were succeeded in the 1940s and 1950s by 'hostess gowns'. Today, loungewear is a growing sector of the fashion market.

Chemise
Linen with muslin frill, inscribed
in ink 'M.J. Sanderson 3 1851'
Britain, 1851
V&A: T.148–1961
Given by Miss P. Canton

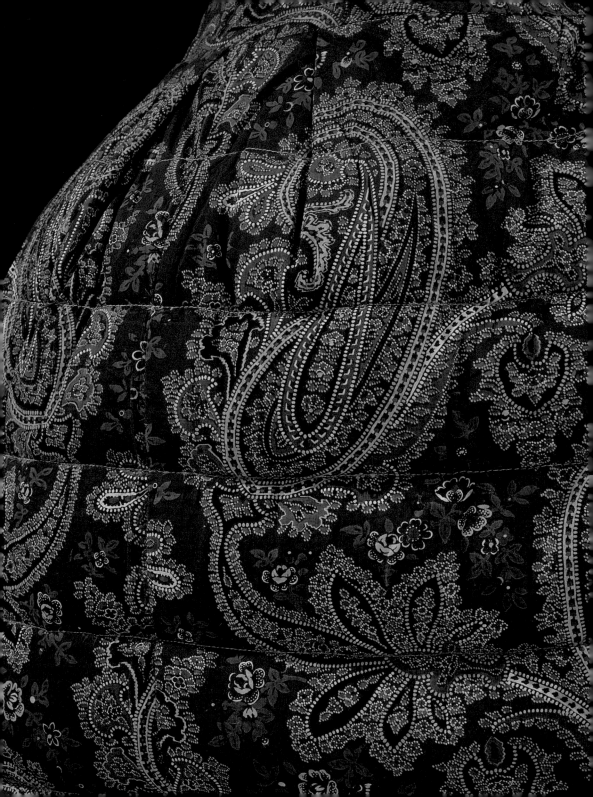

**Petticoat manufactured
by Booth & Fox**
Printed cotton, lined with cotton
and filled with goose down
Britain (London) and Ireland
(Cork), *c*.1860
V&A: T.212–1962
Given by Mrs I. Gadsby-Toni

Woman's drawers
Cotton flannel
Britain, 1890–1910
V&A: T.60–2015
Bequeathed by Harry Matthews

The labels on the fabric swatches read:

LIGHT QUALITY
TRICOT
C 11
IVORY 3

LIGHT QUALITY
TRICOT
C 11
FLESH 70

LIGHT QUALITY
TRICOT
C 11
SKY 71

LIGHT QUALITY
TRICOT
C 11
LILAC 39

Shade card for British Celanese Ltd
Knitted Celanese
Britain, 1924
V&A: AAD/1998/14/26
Given by Marjorie and
Elizabeth Janko

**Sports bra designed
by Marks & Spencer**
Tactel (nylon) and cotton
Britain, 1996
V&A: T.498–1996
Given by the company

**'Shorty' brief
designed by DaDa**
Bamboo, organic cotton and elastane
Britain (Edinburgh and London)
and Sri Lanka (made)
V&A: T.118–2015
Given by the company

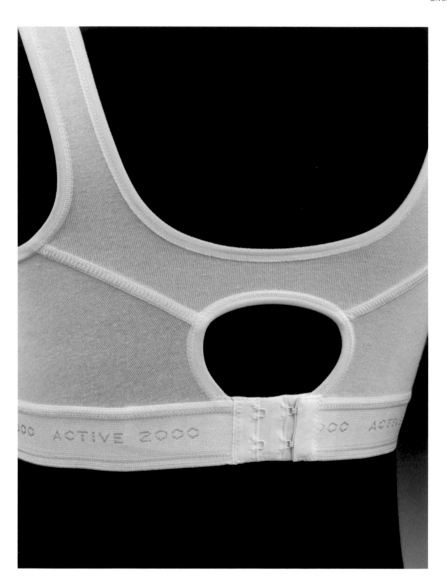

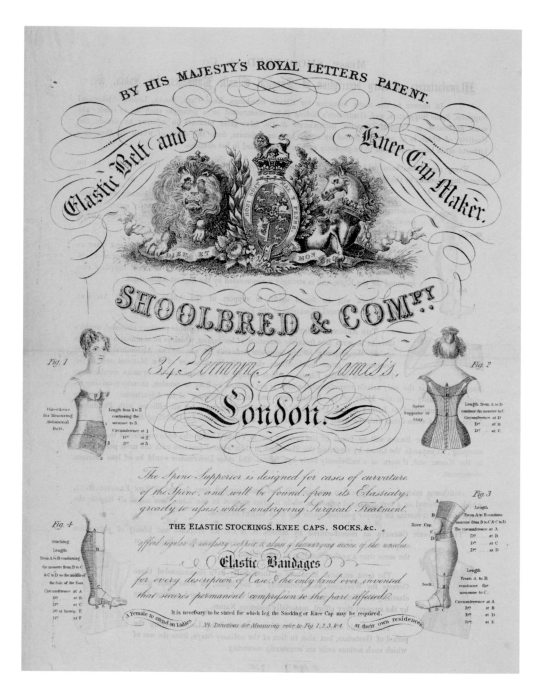

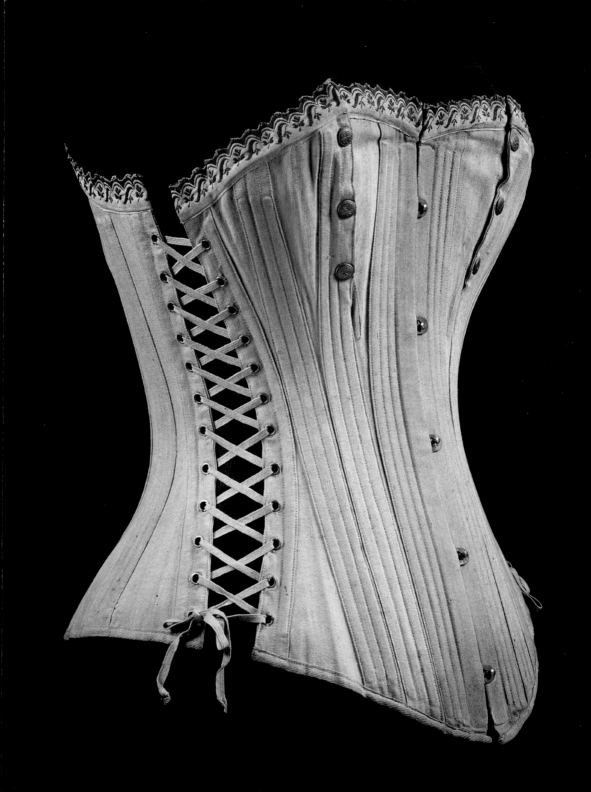

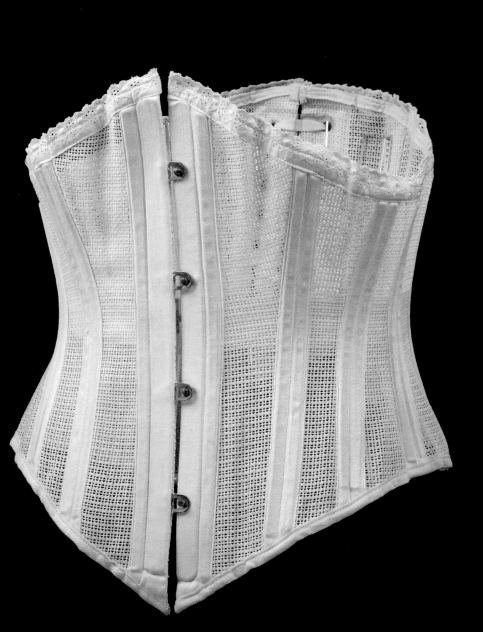

Austerity corset
Paper twine with metal bones
and busk, woven silk and linen
ribbon edging
Austria or Germany, *c.*1917
V&A: T.44–2015

Man's dressing gown
Printed cotton
Britain, *c.*1840
V&A: T.134–1967
Given by Mrs E. Alliot

**Tea gown designed and
made by Liberty & Co. Ltd**
Silk and cotton brocade,
silk satin and silk velvet
Britain (London), *c.*1897
V&A: T.57–1976

**Lounge pyjamas
(jacket, vest and trousers)**
Embroidered silk
China for the European market,
1926–30
V&A: FE.3:1,2&3–2013
Given by Paulus Thomson

Hostess gown
Silk and machine-made lace
France, c.1946
V&A: T.254–1990
Given by Mrs Winifred Le Roy

Kaftan
Silk, organza and satin
Britain, 1970s
V&A: T.133–1990
Given by Sir Anthony Nutting,
'in ever loving memory of my
beloved wife Annie (Anne Gunning)'

**Top and pants
designed by Sibling**
Viscose, nylon, elastane and
metallised fibre
Britain (designed) and China
(made), Spring/Summer 2013
V&A: T.86:1&2-2015
Given by Charlie Porter

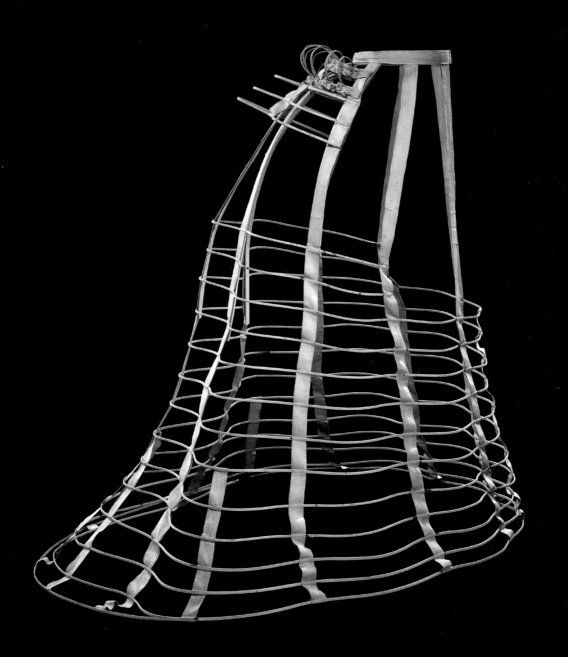

CHAPTER 2 **Shapeshifters**

**Cage crinoline,
the 'Princess Louise
Jupon Patent'**
Linen and spring steel
Britain, c.1871
V&A: T.195–1984
Given by Miss C.E. and E.C. Edlmann

Fashion and underwear are intimately connected. One of underwear's primary roles is to smooth, firm and mould the body in accordance with the fashionable ideal and to provide a substructure for the fashions of the day.

Structural garments such as corsets, crinolines, bustles and bras have also been devised to lift, separate and exaggerate parts of the female anatomy, particularly the breasts, rear and hips. This creates a gendered silhouette that emphasizes the sexual characteristics of a woman's body. When a more androgynous figure is in vogue, as in the 1920s, the role of underwear is to suppress and streamline the female curves.

The materials and construction of shaping and supporting garments affect the wearer's posture, movement and gait. While the corset held the back straight and the buoyancy of the crinoline heightened the sway of the hips, they compromised mobility. Male underwear has also been designed to enhance. Its emphasis on fit draws attention to the linearity of the masculine body while allowing for the curves of the buttocks and sexual organs. Body belts were worn to trim the waist and firm the belly until the 1950s, while contemporary shape wear is designed to support and lift the backside and shape and augment the appearance of the genitals.

However, some types of underwear have been criticized for being over-sexualized, uncomfortable and unhygienic. Just as many women today refuse to wear thongs and push-up bras, a group of women in the nineteenth century rejected boned corsets, crinolines and bustles for damaging the internal organs and distorting the natural proportions of the female body.

**Stays, shift and hoop
made by Andrew Schabner**
Stays: silk damask, lined with linen
and stiffened with whalebone /
Shift: linen / Hoop: linen and cane
Britain, 1740–85
V&A: T.909–1913; T.26–1969; T.120–1969
Given by Messrs Harrods; from the
family of Mrs Deborah Carter,
given by Mr and Mrs R.C. Carter

Corset
Corded and quilted cotton,
silk thread and whalebone
Britain, 1825–35
V&A: T.57–1948

Stays
Cotton lined with linen,
whalebone, silk embroidery
and ribbon lacing
Britain or France, *c*.1800
V&A: T.237–1983

45

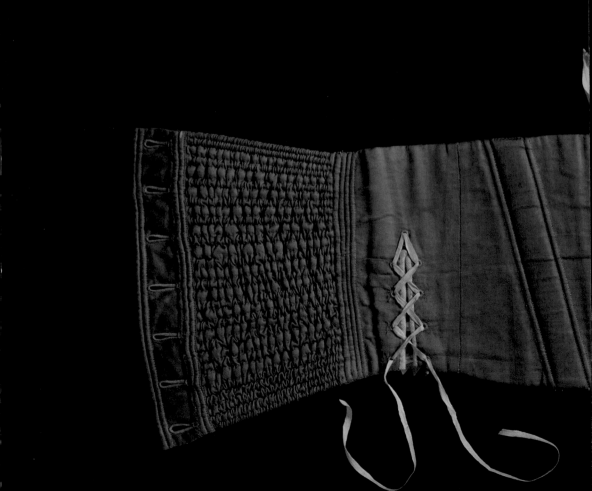

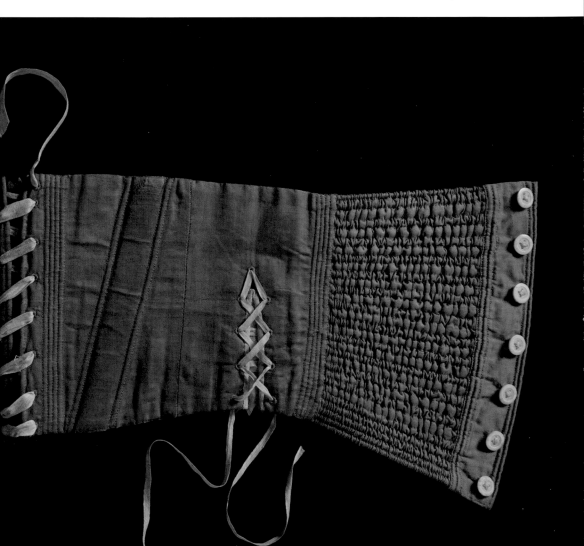

Corset
Silk lined with cotton twill,
whalebone, metal busk and
machine-made lace edging
Britain or France, *c.*1864
V&A: T.169–1961
Given by the Burrows family

Opposite
Crinolette
Cotton and spring steel
with braid edging
Britain, *c.*1870
V&A: T.775C–1913
Given by Messrs Harrods Ltd

Overleaf
Bustle
Crinoline (horsehair woven
with linen), spring steel
Britain, 1870–5
V&A: T.168–1937
Given by Miss Barbara V. Cooper

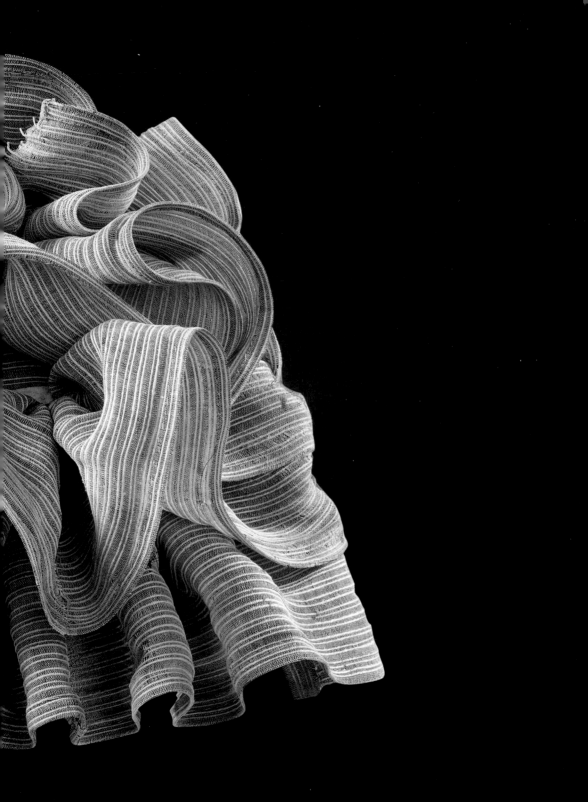

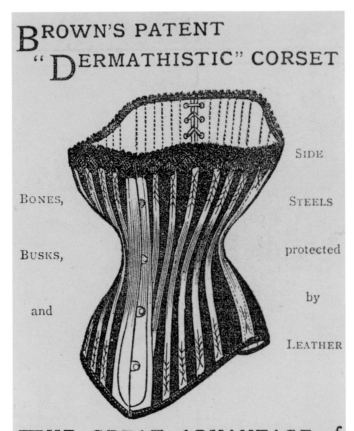

BROWN'S PATENT "DERMATHISTIC" CORSET

BONES,

BUSKS,

and

SIDE

STEELS

protected

by

LEATHER

THE GREAT ADVANTAGE of this PATENT is that the most vulnerable parts of a CORSET have a protecting facing of the Finest Leather, which, to a remarkable degree, increases the durability and strength, besides being a great additional support to the wearer. The great demand for this Corset, and its well merited success, have caused several spurious and worthless imitations to be offered to the public. Ladies are therefore requested to see that each pair is stamped 'BROWN'S PATENT "DERMATHISTIC" on the Busk. To be obtained from all respectable Drapers and Ladies' Outfitters throughout the kingdom, through the principal Wholesale Houses. Price from 5s. 11d. in all colours.

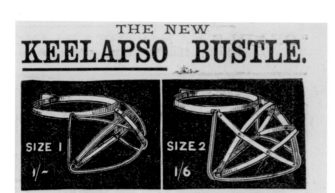

THE NEW KEELAPSO BUSTLE.

SIZE 1	SIZE 2
1/-	1/6

(Regd.)   Patent applied for.

Now she wears the "Keelapso" Bustle and sits down comfortably.

She used to sit like this.

Ever since ladies first began to wear Bustles they have searched in vain for a Bustle in which they could feel at ease. Many of those hitherto used have been simply instruments of torture.

The "Keelapso" Bustle is LIGHT (weighing under 4 oz.), COOL, WELL-FITTING, and CORRECT IN SHAPE; it is firm enough to hold the heaviest garments without crushing. It COLLAPSES ENTIRELY when the wearer sits down, and, when rising, instantly resumes its proper shape, and is so easy and comfortable that **she forgets she is wearing a Bustle at all.** Beware of spurious imitations, and see that every one is stamped "KEELAPSO." Of all Drapers and Ladies' Outfitters.

Price—Size 1 (or smaller size 0), 1s.; Size 2, 1s. 6d.
Post-free, 3d. extra. Send stamps or Postal Order.
Wholesale only of the Manufacturers,

STAPLEY & SMITH, London Wall, London.

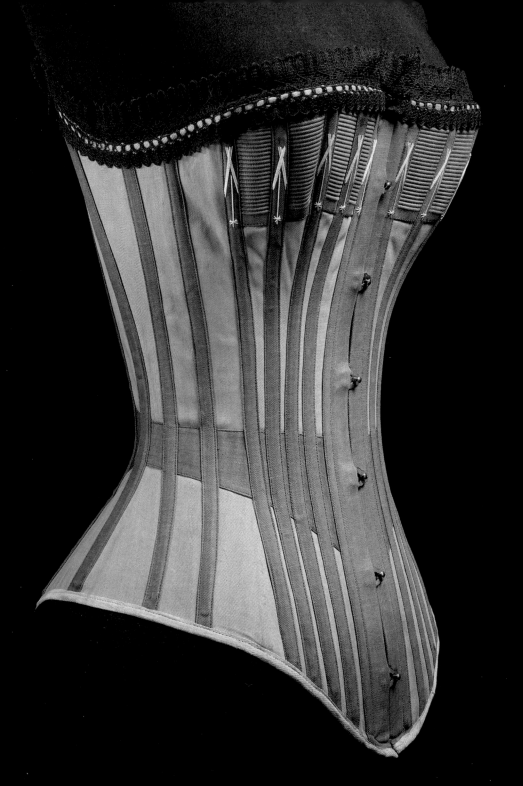

Corset
Cotton, whalebone, metal busk
and machine-made cotton lace
trimming
Germany or Britain, c.1890
V&A: T.90&A–1984
Given by the family of Myer Yanovsky

'Torso of the Statue of Venus of Milo'
and 'Paris Fashion, May, 1880'
William Henry Flower, *Fashion in Deformity:*
as illustrated in the customs of barbarous
and civilised races
Britain (London), 1881
NAL

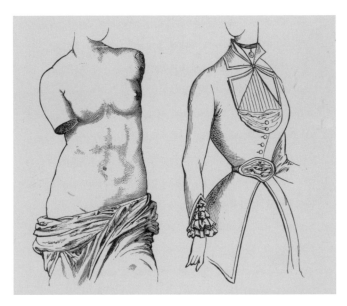

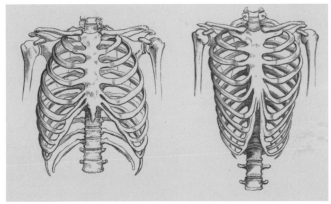

Opposite
'Bust Extender'
manufactured by
The Spirella Corset Company
Cotton, spiral steel bones and
machine-made cotton lace edging
Britain, 1910–14
V&A: T.348–1996
Given by Mrs Jean Murray Muir

Below
'Peter Pan Hidden Treasure' bra
manufactured by Henry Plehn
Longline overwire bra (style 47–3)
with patented 4-section padded cups
Nylon, elastic and foam
USA (New York), *c.*1950
London College of Fashion Archive: 095–29
Given by Lorraine Smith

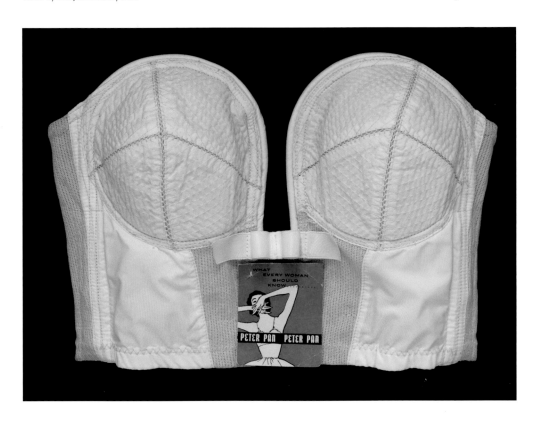

Overleaf
Advertising brochure for the
Charnaux Patent Corset Co. Ltd
Designed by Sackville Advertising
Service; printed by Percy Lund,
Humphries & Co. Ltd
Letterpress on paper
Britain (London and Bradford), *c.*1936
V&A: AAD/1979/10/254

THE NEW CORSELETTE

is especially designed for the fuller figure. Its latex panels of exceptional tensile strength control the diaphragm, give extra support to the breasts and a firm and graceful line to the figure. This model has been created to give the older woman not only additional comfort and ease, but also to strengthen her abdominal muscles, and so reduce fatigue in daily tasks.

CORSI

It frees her of every conscious restriction and gives the correct fashionable line to her figure. The Charnaux Corselette is very simple to put on, being hooked up at the side. In addition, it has a small length of lacing at the back, adjustable to provide proper control of the diaphragm. It is made in peach-coloured latex with silk cups. Sizes 24″ to 38″ waist measurement.

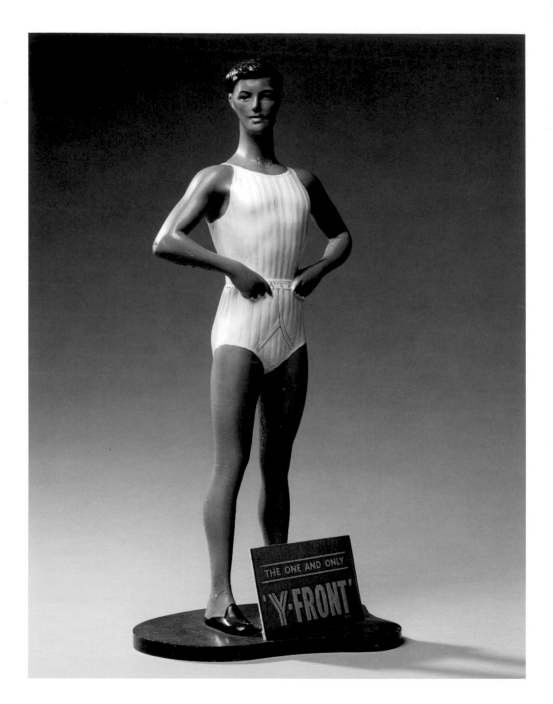

THE ONE AND ONLY
'Y-FRONT'

64

**Display figure and advertising
card for Y-front pants**
Moulded construction;
wooden base; paper card
Probably Britain, 1950s
V&A: T.43:1&2–2015

**Mail order catalogue for
Dean Rogers Ltd, London**
Photography by Charles Whitehorn
Britain (Leavesden), 1970
V&A: Textiles and Fashion collection

CHAPTER 3

Lingerie and Hosiery

Negligée
Silk satin and machine-made lace
France, c.1932
V&A: T.308–1984
Given by Miss J. Bell

Today the term lingerie refers specifically to women's underwear and nightwear, particularly those made from sensual and traditionally luxurious fabrics like satin and lace. However, the root is the French word for linen, *linge*. This robust fabric could be laundered and was used for undergarments worn next to the skin, such as shirts and chemises. In the nineteenth century, lingerie included washable cotton undergarments. The shift in meaning to daintier female items of underclothing came in the late nineteenth century, when delicate lace, embroidery and ribbons began to be used to decorate women's underclothes and silk became an option for the wealthy. Contemporary lingerie is often overtly sexy, creating an interplay between revealing and concealing the body, and designed for seduction.

Hosiery is derived from 'hose', meaning stockings. Until the early seventeenth century, when framework knitting machines came into use in Britain, stockings were hand-knitted or made from woven cloth. Men's and women's stockings were supported by garters, tied around the leg just above or below the knee. Following the invention of suspenders for socks and stockings in the late nineteenth century, garters became more of a female accessory, largely restricted to boudoir and bridal wear.

While Britain had its own hosiery industry, based mainly in London and the Midlands, high-quality products were imported from the sixteenth century. Among these foreign goods were embroidered hand-knitted silk stockings from Spain, luxury items that were still deemed desirable 200 years later. At this time the finest linen came from the Low Countries, especially the Netherlands and Belgium.

Stockings
Knitted silk,
embroidered with silk
Spain, c.1750
V&A: T.156&A–1971
Given by Miss B. Hinton

Below
Garter
Silk inscribed with the words,
'I love not this world in which
thou must not stay, but love
that treasure that abides away.'
Britain, *c.*1750
V&A: T.433–1970
Given by Mr K.L. Stock

Overleaf
Garters
Silk padded with wool,
embroidered with silk
Britain, 1750–1800
V&A: Circ.217&A–1920

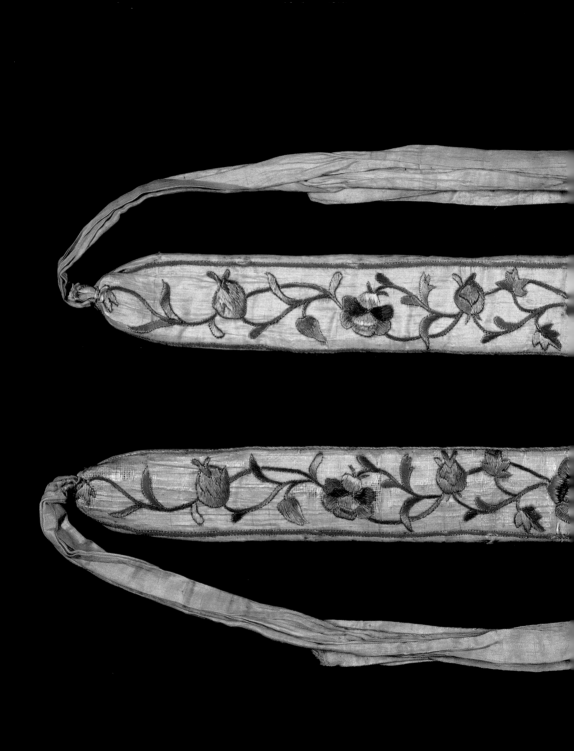

**Stocking worn by
Queen Alexandra
(1844–1925)**
Knitted silk, embroidered
with silk
Britain, *c.*1900
V&A: T.15–1956
Given by Mrs Horton

**Stocking exhibited at the
1900 Universal Exhibition,
Paris**
Knitted silk embroidered with
silk, beads and sequins
France, *c.*1900
V&A: T.53–1962
Given by the Dowager
Lady Swaythling

Dress shirt
Linen, embroidered with
cotton thread
Britain, *c.*1850-60
V&A: 1112–1904

Corset
Silk satin, lace and whalebone
with a steel busk and metal eyelets
Probably Britain, 1890–5
V&A: T.738–1974

Princess petticoat
Cotton lawn, machine-made lace
and silk ribbon
Britain, *c*.1905
V&A: T.61–1973
Given by Major and Mrs Broughton

Bust bodice
retailed by Dickins and Jones
Machine-made lace, figured silk
ribbon with boning
Britain (London), c.1901
V&A: T.33–1996
Given by Christina McMillan

Homemade brassiere
Silk satin and machine-made lace
Britain, c.1925–30
V&A: T.368–1976
Given by Mrs A. Lu

**Wedding camisole
designed by Hermine Ltd**
Silk chiffon and machine-made
lace with silk embroidery
Britain (London), 1932
V&A: T.227–1969
Worn and given by Mrs Joan Acton

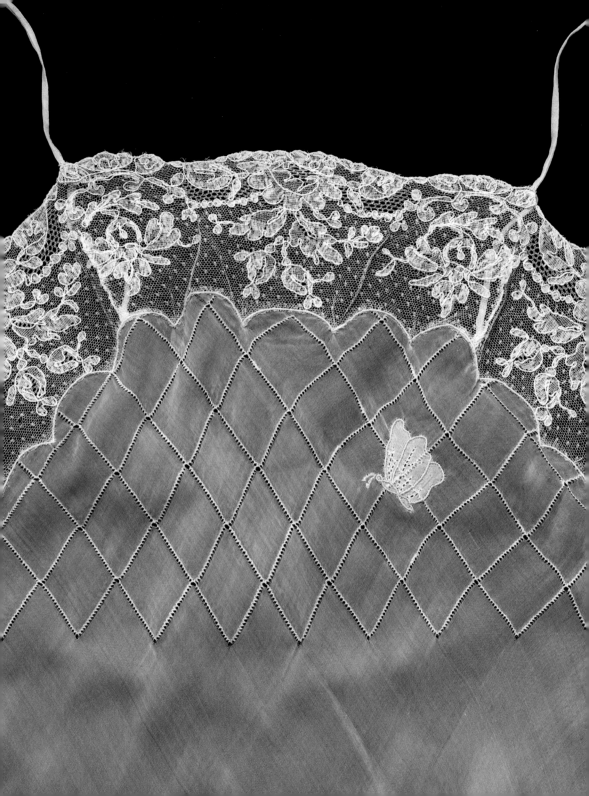

Knickers
Silk chiffon with machine-made
lace made by a Russian lingerie
company, possibly Hitrovo
Probably France (Paris), 1930s
Photographer: Tessa Hallmann
The Royal Pavilion & Museums,
Brighton & Hove: CT001074.2

**Nightdress attributed
to Lucile (1863–1935)**
Silk crêpe and machine-made lace
Britain (London), 1913
V&A: T.1–1973
Given by Mrs Wormald

Nightdress
Silk crêpe-de-chine with silk
appliqué and embroidery
France (Paris), c.1935
V&A: T.309–1984
Given by Miss J. Bell

**Nightdress designed by
Thea Scott (fl.1937–61)**
Silk chiffon trimmed with
machine-made lace and satin ribbon
Britain (London), c.1951–3
V&A: T.329–1987
Given by Coral Browne

Opposite
Slip
Silk chiffon and ribbon
with machine-made lace
Britain, *c.*1960
V&A: T.153–1998

Overleaf
**Knickers and puff sleeves,
'Rosette Cheeks (Exploded
and Capped)', designed by
Strumpet & Pink**
Silk chiffon and silk satin ribbon
Scotland (Edinburgh), 2011
V&A: T.115:1, 2&3–2012
Given by the designers

'Tamila' lingerie set from the
Agent Provocateur Soirée collection
Machine-made lace (polyamide, viscose, silk and elastane)
Britain (London) and Romania, Spring/Summer 2015
Photographer: Sebastian Faena
Model: Eniko Mihalik

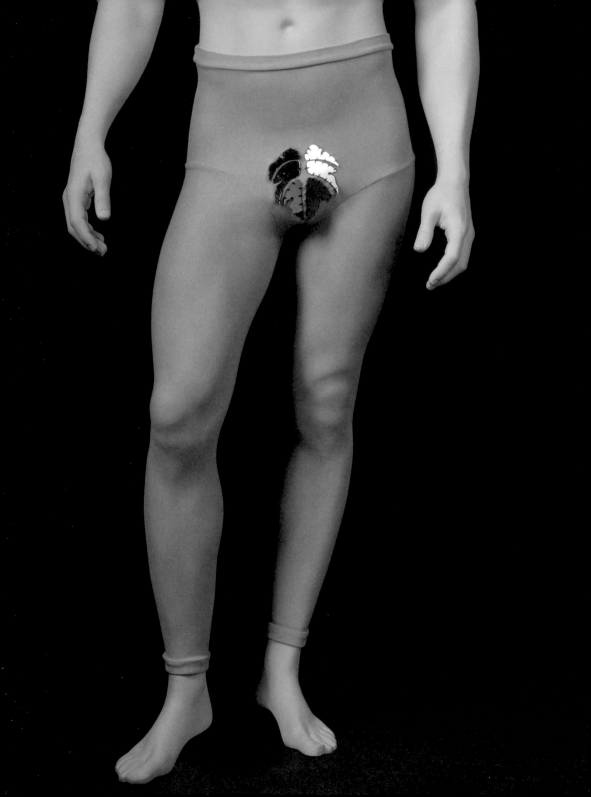

CHAPTER 4 **Revelation and Transformation**

**Leggings designed
by Vivienne Westwood
(b.1941)**
Nylon, spandex and mirror glass
Britain (London),
Autumn/Winter 1989–90
Photographer: Brian Sanderson
Fashion Institute of Design and
Marketing, Los Angeles: 2003.5.13

Vivienne Westwood's ironic and provocative use of a mirrored glass fig leaf to decorate flesh-coloured leggings in 1989 is a reminder of the story of Adam and Eve and the Christian association of nudity with sin and shame. It is also an example of the way in which post-war and contemporary fashion designers have experimented with underwear to explore the physical and cultural aspects of the body and push the boundaries between private and public.

Shirts, chemises and petticoats were sometimes partially revealed before the twentieth century. The motivation was usually to show the quality of the underwear or, in the case of muslin dresses, to highlight the transparency of this expensive fabric and so indicate the wearer's wealth. However, by the late twentieth century the radical, transgressive clothes worn by punks and in London's clubs were a key influence on avant-garde fashion designers. Many used visible underwear to excite controversy and challenge conventional attitudes to nudity, sexuality and gender. Corsetry in particular was favoured for its twentieth-century associations with fetish and pornography.

Historical costume has also been an important resource for designers, presenting corsetry in a different context. The effect of corsets, crinolines and bustles on the proportions and movement of the body and their diverse materials and construction afford many opportunities for probing the relationship between body and clothing. They are also invested with a theatricality that makes them an arresting sight on the catwalk and particularly seductive for designers interested in performance and display.

**Unknown printmaker after
James Gillray (1757–1815)**
*The Graces in a high Wind – a Scene
taken from Nature, in Kensington
Gardens,* published by McCleary
Hand-coloured etching
Britain (London) and Ireland
(Dublin), 1810
V&A: E.510–1955

**Dress and knickers
designed by John Galliano
(b.1960) for Givenchy**
Dress: muslin embroidered with silk;
knickers: machine-made lace
France (Paris), Spring/Summer
1996 haute couture
Model: Nadja Auermann
From *L'Officiel 1000 modèles,* 1996

**Evening dress and petticoat
designed by Antonio Castillo
(1904–84) for Lanvin**
Dress: net appliquéd with wool
felt spots trimmed with silk satin
ribbon; petticoat: stiffened net,
gauze and nylon crin with a
boned foundation
France (Paris), 1957
V&A: T.526A–1974
Given by Lady Stella Ednam

**Lingerie dress
designed by Elie Saab (b.1964)**
Silk and machine-made lace
France (Paris), Spring/Summer
2011 *haute couture*
Worn by Mila Kunis at the
83rd Annual Academy Awards,
Los Angeles, 27 February 2011
Photographer: Steve Granitz

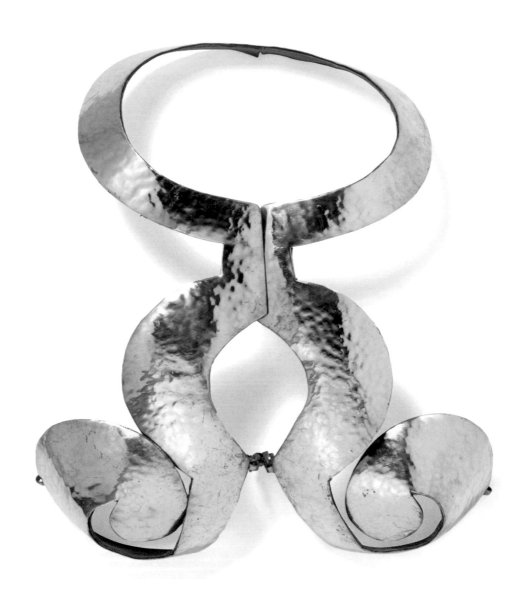

**Bra designed and made
by Helen Newman (b.1940)**
Beaten brass lined with suede
Britain, 1970
V&A: M.8:1–2006

**Dress designed by Jean
Paul Gaultier (b.1952)**
Silk, machine-made lace
and beaded fringe
France (Paris) (designed)
and Italy (made), 1989
V&A: T.114–2009

**Fig leaf for the cast of *David*,
after the marble original by
Michelangelo (1475–1564),
probably made by
D. Brucciani & Co.**
Plaster
Probably Britain, *c.*1857
V&A: REPRO.1857A–161

Jennie Baptiste (b.1971)
Brixton Boyz
Lith print
Britain (London), 2001
V&A: E.971–2010
Purchase supported by the
National Lottery through the
Heritage Lottery Fund

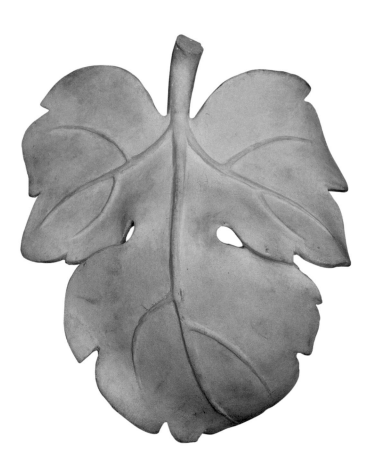

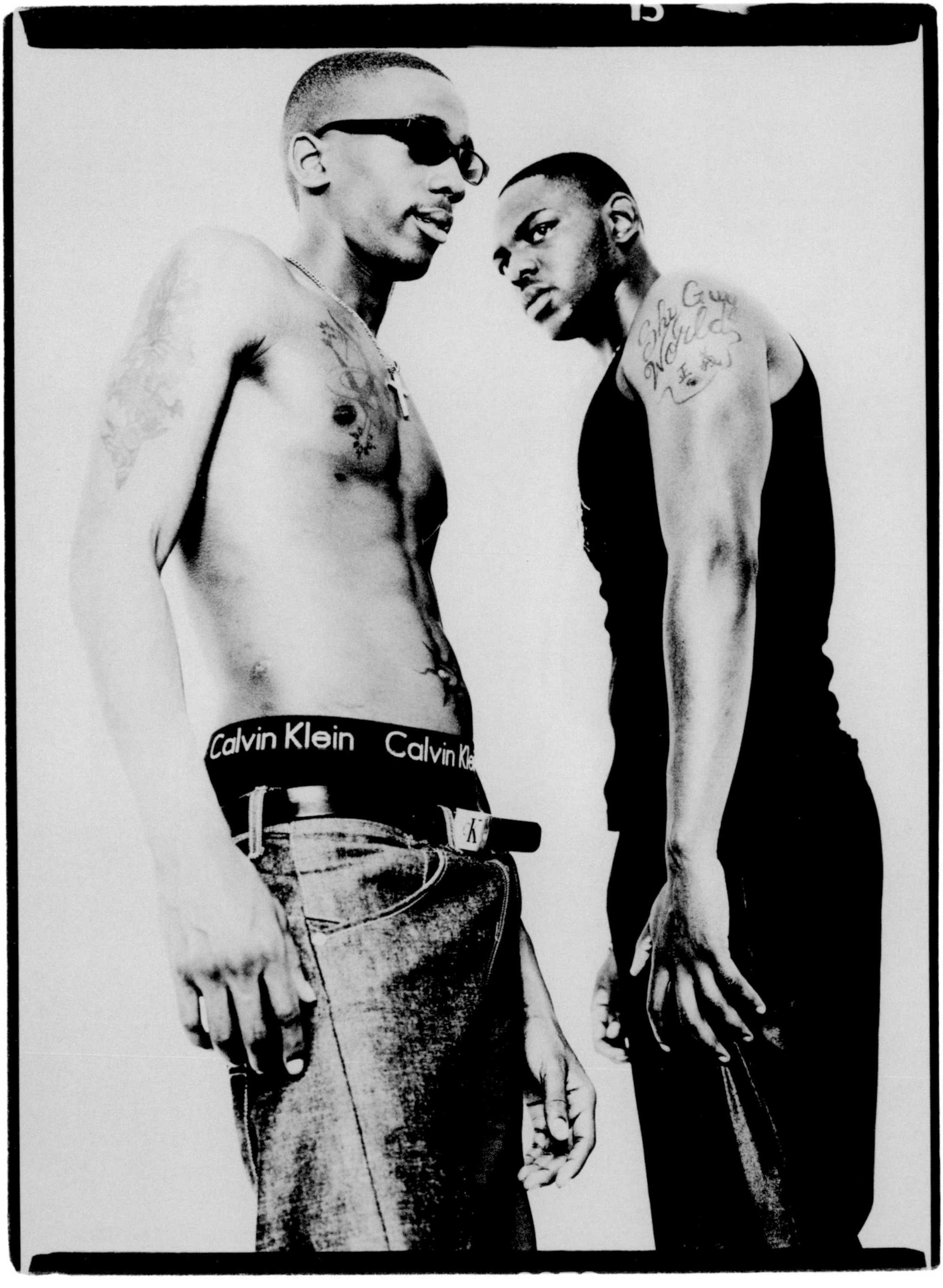
15
Calvin Klein
Calvin Kle

Trompe l'oeil corset dress designed Antonio Berardi (b.1968)
Rayon and elastane
Britain (London),
Spring/Summer 2009
Worn by Gwyneth Paltrow
for the premiere of *Two Lovers*,
Paris, 4 November 2008
Photographer: Michel Dufour

Shibari girdle dress (with detachable collar and garters) by Atelier Bordelle
Satin elastic bands, silk satin and
gold lurex lace, with gold-plated
rings and sliders and zip fastening
Britain (London),
Autumn/Winter 2016–17
Photographer: Benjamin Kauffmann
Model: Ema Kovac

**Wicker dress designed
by Dolce & Gabbana**
Silk, stretch nylon and wicker
Italy, Spring/Summer 2013
ready-to-wear
Photographer: Yannis Vlamos
Model: Zuzanna Bijoch

Further Reading

Denis Bruna, ed., *Fashioning the Body: an intimate history
    of the silhouette* (New Haven, 2015)
Emily Campbell and Alice Cicolini, *Inside Out: underwear
    and style in the UK* (London, 2000)
Alison Carter, *Underwear: The Fashion History* (New York, 1992)
Shaun Cole, *The Story of Men's Underwear* (New York, 2010)
Patricia A. Cunningham, *Reforming Women's Fashion 1850-1920:
    Politics, Health, and Art* (Ohio, 2003)
C. Willett and Phillis Cunnington, *The History of Underclothes*
    (London, 1951)
Elizabeth Ewing, *Dress and Undress: A history of women's
    underwear* (London, 1989)
Jane Farrell-Beck and Colleen Gau, *Uplift: The Bra in America*
    (Philadelphia, 2002)
Deborah Jaffé, *Ingenious Women from Tincture of Saffron
    to Flying Machines* (Stroud, 2004)
Paul Jobling, *Advertising Menswear: masculinity and fashion
    in the British media since 1945* (London and New York, 2014)
Sarah Levitt, *Victorians Unbuttoned* (London, 1986)
Eleri Lynn, *Underwear Fashion in Detail* (London, 2010)
Colin McDowell, *The Anatomy of Fashion: Why We Dress
    the Way We Do* (London, 2013)
Stella Mary Newton, *Health, Art and Reason: Dress Reformers
    of the Nineteenth Century* (London, 1974)
Lynn Sorge-English, *Stays and Body Image in London:
    The Staymaking Trade, 1680–1810 (The Body, Gender
    and Culture, Number 6)*, (London, 2011)

Picture Credits

666 857

Acknowledgements

This book has been written in association with the exhibition *Undressed: A Brief History of Underwear.* I would like to express my gratitude to the exhibition sponsors Agent Provocateur and Revlon and to all those who have kindly donated or lent clothing to the exhibition for their generous support.

Particular thanks are due to Joanna Norman, Susanna Cordner, Cassie Davies-Strodder and Susan North for their perceptive and helpful comments on the text, to Christopher Marsden and staff at the Archive of Art and Design, to Richard Davis and Jaron James for photography, to Lilia Prier-Tidsall in Textile Conservation and Charlotte Hubbard in Sculpture Conservation for preparing objects for photography and to Hanne Faurby for coordinating it. Thanks are also due to Esme Hawes and Ellie Porter for their research and enthusiasm for the project.

I would also like to acknowledge the scholarship and contribution of Eleri Lynn, the author of *Underwear Fashion in Detail* and curator of the touring exhibition which preceded this larger show.

I am grateful to Zara Anvari for her editorial skills, to Clare Davis for her production expertise and to Maggi Smith for designing the book.